Why Must I Cry?

Why Must I Cry?

KAYLA D. JOHNSON

"Weeping May endure for a night but joy comes in the morning."
Psalms 30:5b

iUniverse, Inc.
Bloomington

Why Must I Cry?

iUniverse books may be ordered through booksellers or by contacting:

iUniverse
1663 Liberty Drive
Bloomington, IN 47403
www.iuniverse.com
1-800-Authors (1-800-288-4677)

ISBN: 978-1-4620-5026-0 (sc)
ISBN: 978-1-4620-5028-4 (hc)
ISBN: 978-1-4620-5027-7 (ebk)

Printed in the United States of America

iUniverse rev. date: 09/13/2011

Contents

Dedicated to:

My children: Charlotte, Carla, Marguarite, and Samantha, who suffered much because of all my pain. It is my prayer **that** as I write this book and it brings closure in one area of my life that it will **also** open your lives to living. It is my desire that you will have the courage to walk out your destiny in Him, for you were born for such a time as this. Be courageous for the kingdom of God suffers violence, but the violent take it by force. You have been given a legacy by your heavenly Father. Take it and never settle! And to the memory of my earthly father, Samuel Aker, whom I now release so that I too can be free.

Preface

Why Now?

After pondering over telling my story for many years, why now? I suppose in every life there comes a point when enough is enough. I had gone through many years (in fact, most of my life) feeling angry, afraid and pretending I was making lemonade out of lemons, when the reality was, that there was very little sugar. I was seeing so many women feeling pitiful when they had the ability to be powerful. I wanted to shout, "Stop letting the enemy make you hold on to what you can't change. I have been there. Please turn around." I felt like I was crying in the dark and no one could hear. I saw people close to me heading down a road I had already been and it wasn't good. I had this stirring in my spirit telling me, "Go and give them that which I have given you."

Then I had to battle an attack on my health. Thank God for Proverbs 4:20-22. I made it my own. It says, "My son, give attention to my words; Incline your ear to my sayings. Do not let them depart from your eyes; Keep them in the midst of your heart; For they *are* life to those who find them, And *health* to all their flesh." What God had given me was his Word. I had to not let his Word depart from me. His Word is medicine. It will cure wherever it hurts. It works for emotional healing as well as physical healing. But the Word only works if you work it.

Children of God, it is time to fight back. The season of restoration is now. Time to go boldly into the enemy's camp and take back the life and hope he has stolen from you. How has he gotten away with it so long? With guilt! Don't live with past guilt. It is a weapon that cannot prosper against you. Child of God, you have been given the "Word." Romans 8:1-3 says, "There is therefore now no condemnation for those who are in Christ Jesus, who do not walk according to the flesh, but according to the Spirit. For the law of the Spirit of life in Christ Jesus has made me free from the law of sin and death.

For what the law could not do in that it was weak through the flesh, God did by sending His own son in the likeness of sinful flesh, on account of sin: He condemned sin in the flesh." Don't keep trying to pay a debt that has already been canceled. So, that's why now; because I cry.

I cry for the children who were molested and who blame themselves, thinking they must have done something wrong. I cry for the child abused, who grows up thinking beatings represent love. I cry for the woman raped and the wife beaten who doesn't know how to escape. I cry for the child told he was a mistake and whose hope has been shattered. I cry for the drug addict looking for a fix and the drunk looking for the next drink. I cry for all the reasons they are seeking to forget. I cry for the motherless and the fatherless. I cry for the mother who can't feed her children and the father who won't come home. I cry for the homeless seeking refuge wherever they can find it. I cry because I can no longer keep silent. I cry for those who share my story. Take this journey through the pages with me as we make the crooked road straight and together we will go from mourning to laughter.

Acknowledgements

I want to first acknowledge God, my heavenly Father. Thank you for showing me the right relationship of a father to a daughter. I thank you Jesus for loving me despite myself and pleading my cause. I thank the precious Holy Spirit for teaching me how to be all right with myself and to allow him to develop my gifts, and better understand that broken vessels can be mended.

It is a blessing to have my husband Alvin in my life loving me unconditionally and encouraging me to keep getting up. He is my confidant and my best friend, whom I love dearly.

I thank God for being blessed with four amazing daughters, who have loved their mother through all her mistakes and trials. They have given me the courage to write this book. I love you Charlotte, Carla, Marguarite and Samantha; you are the jewels in my crown.

There are so many who have cried and laughed with me. To you, I say thank you:

Hilda Aker, thanks for taking me in when I had nowhere to go. Also for saying, "You go girl," When I wanted to give up.

Lottie Tucker, you taught me the importance of learning. Thanks for all the hours you invested in me, instilling confidence in my abilities.

Jarvis Wooten, my cousin, who by example showed me the true meaning of family. You will never understand how much you truly mean to me.

My Aunt, Mattie Streeter, just for being there. For all the hugs, prayers and faith **in believing** that I could make it. My childhood would have been unbearable without you. Words can't express how I feel. I'll simply say, "Thank you."

Robert Hughes, who taught me that love was possible and could be beautiful. You will always hold a place in my heart.

Alice Jones, my "Childhood" friend, your godchild, and I thank you.

Tony & Loretta, I am grateful for what you did for me and my children. May your unselfishness come back to you a hundred fold.

Cynthia Wilson, for all the times you shook me and told me to "Get tough," for being like a sister to me, and for being there when I felt alone. I can never repay you or Raymond.

Lynda McCartney, for being a friend with no strings attached. For always having the right word at the right time and for reminding me that I am valuable.

Roxanne Graham, for always having a listening ear and never judging me. You are a constant friend. Thanks for all the sacrifices to help fulfill the call on my life.

Charles and Dorothy Williams, you have inspired my life in so many ways. Thank you for feeling like parents to me. Your words of encouragement and faith in my gifts made me feel like, despite the obstacles, I could run on. I could not love or appreciate you more than I do now.

Frank & Ruth Murphy, thank you for all your spiritual counseling and being there for me. Thanks for telling me what I needed to hear even when I didn't want to hear it.

Margaret Greene, who I have loved like a daughter, I miss your homemade cookies, the prayers and all the fun times. You will always be special to me.

Pastor Terry & Debra Howell, who I love dearly, thank you for teaching me what forgiveness and God's love looks like.

And certainly **last but** not least, my Pastors, Earl & Linda Brown, who knowing all my challenges, still believed in me. Thank you for teaching by example. Your guidance has led me to this road in my journey; one, which I pray, will leave a few less souls crying in the dark.

Introduction

'Why Must I Cry' is about gaining strength and endurance in the midst of your trials and pain. Life is full of ups and downs but you don't let them determine your joy or your future. I make known to you my personal failures and my personal painful experiences that I've had to struggle with in life, but I made a decision to move forward and to release those things which were holding me captive.

This book brings out a lot of memories from my past, but it is all for a purpose. My purpose is to let you know that no matter what you struggled with in your past, you can be free from those harsh and painful thoughts and feelings. I explain how you can do this and how you too can make a positive turnaround in your life. I bring revelation to you in ways you never thought were possible. Just by allowing the truth that I'm about to unveil to you, you will see how everything is *possible.*

This book is about understanding how you can be free from your hurts that you believe will always be with you and will always keep you the way you are. You will learn how to fight for what belongs to you. It's about truth . . . the inspiring Word of God . . . and the hope, love, peace, and satisfaction that comes from Him. The writing let's you know that no one is perfect and that everyone can eventually see a light at the end of the tunnel.

You will learn that you are not alone in your situation. Inspirational truth is here to grasp your thoughts and help you make changes within yourself to become a better you. I talk about not one, but many issues that affected me in many ways. If I had listened to that evil, negative, unconstructive, unhelpful, pessimistic, harmful and depressing voice, I would not be writing to you right now. These pages will bring life to your situation and encourage you to live the life that you were intended to live free from fear of the past.

When you feel like giving up, remember why you held on for so long in the first place.

Author Unknown

CHAPTER ONE

Thanksgiving Day

Chapter One

Thanksgiving Day

"Only fear the Lord, and serve Him in truth with all your heart; for consider what great things He has done for you." 1 Samuel 12:24.

The smell of sweet potato pies, sound of children playing and laughter filled the room. It was Thanksgiving. I ask very little of my girls, but Thanksgiving Day is the one time I want them all to come home. And not only do we get a chance to find out what is going on in each others lives, but it is when the truth comes out. Now that they are grown they tell on each other things Mom didn't know. They feel that it's too late for Mom to punish them now.

The kitchen is the hangout as I'm basting the turkey, potatoes are being peeled, and macaroni and cheese is being made. Seeing the girls and the grandkids laughing does my heart good. "Mama," one of them said. "Remember when you were up praying one night that somehow God would provide gas for you to go to work and make it back home the next day? And you woke up the following morning yelling, 'Praise God, Glory Hallelujah. God is good!" because miraculously you had a full tank?" (Of course, who would forget a miracle like that?) "Well, those two over there," referring to the two older sisters, "snuck out of the house while you were sleeping, and with a boyfriend at that. They went joy riding half the night in your car and then their friend filled it up with a tank of gas. And the next day you were just praising God about how He provided." They laughed thinking they had gotten one over on Mom. And I told them "You may have thought you were being smart, but He still provided."

I then listened to one sister tell the other, "And you still haven't changed a bit, you still tell Mama everything." I watched them go back and forth about who had the biggest mouth and thought about my own childhood and how I wished I had more fun and pleasant memories than not. Despite my childhood, however, I was seeing what great things God had done through my children.

I had grown up in an upper middle class family. My father was a career soldier in the army. I had two brothers, one sister and a mom whom we thought was the best cook in the world. Being a military family we seemed to always be moving. We had lived in Germany and more places in the States than I can remember. I even have a brother that was born in Guam. Perhaps our moving so often is why all the interruptions in my own life, after a while, just seemed normal.

My father's favorite breakfast was vodka and orange juice with a camel cigarette. I don't think I can ever remember him not drinking. Most of my memories of him were very painful. I am sure he was fighting his own demons. No one drinks that much unless you are trying to forget something. I know that my father had the desire to love and give love but you can't give what you yourself don't have. The void in his life created one in ours as well.

I never once heard my father mention the Name of God. It is difficult to be able to relate to the love of a Heavenly Father when your perception of your earthy father is so distorted. A father should represent love, security, and protection. In fact, God created us for love so we would have a natural yearning to be accepted and loved. When we don't get that from our father or when there is no father present to give it, we grow up with love deficits. We have a void and a sense of something missing in our lives and a need to fill it with something. That search for fulfillment can be costly. I remembered empty relationships because I so desperately wanted to feel loved. What was sad is I really didn't know what love was. It is frustrating to be in search for something and not know what it feels like. If you don't know how it feels then how will you know if you find it? I think in the core of my heart was just the desire to feel accepted. Perhaps that is why I was so good in the Drama Club, it always felt good to be anybody but me. I know now it is because I had never been introduced to the real me.

But today, Thanksgiving day, I was seeing my own family enjoying what we had worked hard to achieve even though the odds were stacked against us. Thank God for Romans 8:31, "What then shall we then say to these things? If God is for us, who can be against us?" There is so much power in trusting God when the deck is stacked against you. My struggles and pain without God's grace would have been my only legacy to my children. Thank God He had better plans for me and for them.

Jeremiah 1:5-8, "Before I formed you in the womb, I knew you; Before you were born I sanctified you; I ordained you a prophet to the nations." Then said I: "Ah, Lord God! Behold, I cannot speak, for I am a youth." But the Lord said to me: "Do not say, 'I am a youth,' for you shall go to all to whom I send you, and whatever I command you, you shall speak. Do not be afraid of their faces, for I am with you to deliver you," says the Lord."

Before God created us in our mother's womb he knew us. He knew our hearts, our souls, our characters, and because he knew us, His Spirit and His love gave us what we needed for this life, our gifts, our talents, our characters, our skills, the qualities that we would need to serve Him in this world. He knew our struggles before they came to be.

He already knew this messed up, abused girl would need His grace before I was even a thought to my mom or alcoholic father. That's why I have survived much, for a time such as this. Regardless of what you are facing in your life right now there is a divine plan and a purpose. I promise you God has placed the power to overcome inside you. Trust that His Word will not fail you.

Of course I wouldn't have known very much about trusting in God had it not been for my awesome, awesome Granddaddy. I will never forget him. We used to call him, "Big Daddy." He was a huge statue of a man. He was my mom's dad. They were from Tennessee. I can remember even as a small child waiting for him to come home from work in the evenings and we would run down to the corner store to meet him and he would always have something there special for us. He loved his grandchildren. But he also loved the Lord more than life itself. I can remember even as a child him teaching us how to pray and telling us things that were in the Bible. I really believe that was God, even then, preparing me for all the things that I was going to have to face in my young life; making me strong when I didn't know I was going to have to be strong. It is just so awesome how Abba Father looks after us even when we don't understand what we are in need of.

I remember also how my grandfather would tell us bible stories and we would just feel like we could conquer the giants because they were conquered in the Word of God. And he could make the word of God just seem so real. I learned very young how to get excited about a God no one could defeat and who would always protect you.

I also remember when we moved to Germany away from "Big Daddy," and how much I missed him. I remember just before he died, him coming and visiting me in my room. Of course, no one believed that actually could happen, because he died in Tennessee. But I think that it was just my love for him and God's way of reassuring me that even though my grand father could no longer be with me, that God would always have someone there watching out for me.

I didn't understand at that time how very important it was that I was going to need someone watching over me. I didn't know how much that would mean to me because I didn't have any idea what I was in store for, or how important my attitude as I faced difficult times would be. I once read an article by Francie Baltazar-Schwartz that really blessed me. Let me share that with you before I go further.

Attitude is Everything
By: Francie Baltazar-Schwartz

Jerry was the kind of guy you love to hate. He was always in a good mood and always had something positive to say. When someone would ask him how he was doing, he would reply, "If I were any better, I would be twins!"

He was a unique manager because he had several waiters who had followed him around from restaurant to restaurant. The reason the waiters followed Jerry was because of his attitude. He was a natural motivator. If an employee was having a bad day, Jerry was there telling the employee how to look on the positive side of the situation.

Seeing this style really made me curious, so one day I went up to Jerry and asked him, "I don't get it! You can't be a positive person all of the time. How do you do it?" Jerry replied, "Each morning I wake up and say to myself, Jerry, you have two choices today. You can choose to be in a good mood or you can choose to be in a bad mood." I choose to be in a good mood. Each time something bad happens, I can choose to be a victim or I can choose to learn from it. I choose to learn from it. Every time someone comes to me complaining, I can choose to accept their complaining or I can point out the positive side of life. I choose the positive side of life.

"Yeah, right, it's not that easy," I protested. "Yes it is," Jerry said. "Life is all about choices. When you cut away all the junk, every situation is a choice. You choose how you react to situations. You choose how people will affect your mood. You choose to be in a good mood or bad mood. The bottom line: It's your choice how you live life."

I reflected on what Jerry said. Soon thereafter, I left the restaurant industry to start my own business. We lost touch, but I often thought about him when I made a choice about life instead of reacting to it.

Several years later, I heard that Jerry did something you are never supposed to do in a restaurant business: he left the back door open one morning and was held up at gunpoint by three armed robbers. While trying to open the safe, his hand, shaking from nervousness, slipped off the combination. The robbers panicked and shot him. Luckily, Jerry was found relatively quickly and rushed to the local trauma center. After 18 hours of surgery and weeks of intensive care, Jerry was released from the hospital with fragments of the bullets still in his body.

I saw Jerry about six months after the accident. When I asked him how he was, he replied, "If I were any better, I'd be twins. Wanna see my scars?"

I declined to see his wounds, but did ask him what had gone through his mind as the robbery took place. "The first thing that went through my mind was that I should have locked the back door," Jerry replied. "Then, as I lay on the floor, I remembered that I had two choices: I could choose to live, or I could choose to die. I chose to live."

"Weren't you scared? Did you lose consciousness?" I asked. Jerry continued, "The paramedics were great. They kept telling me I was going to be fine. But when they wheeled me into the emergency room and I saw the expressions on the faces of the doctors and nurses, I got really scared. In their eyes, I read, "He's a dead man." I knew I needed to take action." "What did you do?" I asked.

"Well, there was a big, burly nurse shouting questions at me," said Jerry. "She asked if I was allergic to anything. "Yes," I replied. The doctors and nurses stopped working as they waited for my reply. I took a deep breath and yelled, "Bullets!" Over their laughter, I told them, "I am choosing to live. Operate on me as if I am alive, not dead."

Jerry lived thanks to the skill of his doctors, but also because of his amazing attitude. I learned from him that every day we have the choice to live fully. Attitude, after all, is everything.

Francie Baltazar-Schwartz

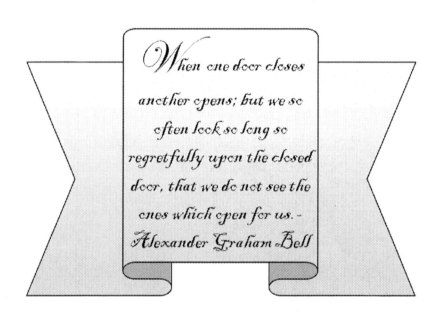

When one door closes another opens; but we so often look so long so regretfully upon the closed door, that we do not see the ones which open for us. - Alexander Graham Bell

CHAPTER TWO

Satan Desires to Sift You

Chapter Two

Satan Desires to Sift You

When I was twelve years old my dad, who was in the military, was stationed at Ft. Jackson, South Carolina. Little did I know it was a place that was going to change the rest of my life. On one particular day Dad didn't have to work and Mom was at work. I wasn't feeling well that day and was left home with my father. It was a beautiful day outside but one that would cause many storms inside my young mind.

I can remember sitting outside our home making paper dolls—the kind that you would open up and they would string all together. I felt like I had really accomplished something being able to make those cute dolls. As I was making them I heard my dad calling me, "Kayla, come here, come here." So I went inside to see what he wanted. I went upstairs. And when I went upstairs I didn't know that when I went into that room my whole life would change in a way that it was never supposed to and I would encounter something that no child should have to ever go through. He had been drinking as always. What was new; one drink after another drink. He forced me to lie down on the bed with him; it was hard to even imagine what was going to happen after that.

After struggling with him trying to touch me in places that I didn't want to be touched and doing things that I just didn't want done to me, I finally broke loose and ran out of the bedroom. I tripped down the stairs as I ran outside. The house sat up on bricks so it was easy for me the get up under the house. I can remember spiders crawling all over my body. But I was more afraid of him than I was of the spiders. He was looking for me. I could hear him calling me, "Kayla, where are you?" I would not answer. I remember sitting there for hours until I finally heard my mom come home.

When I heard her going up the steps and into the house I ran to her and told her what had happened and how he touched me and what he tried to do to me. She was angry. She proceeded up the steps to speak to him about the events that had taken place while she was gone. I could hear them upstairs fussing and arguing until finally she called me and said, "Come here, Kayla." I went upstairs to see what she wanted and she said, "Your dad has something to say to you." He looked at me in his drunkenness and said, "I'm sorry." I felt like, "That's it, that's all?" But I could tell that this wasn't the end. From that day on he would never forgive me for telling Mom.

And I was right, I spent the next few years of my life hiding from him almost nightly, afraid that he would do things that I didn't want done to me. I would find closets or spaces that I could crawl into and lie in the dark. I could hear him walking through the house looking for me, but very quietly because he didn't want mom to know what he was doing. But he didn't find me. I learned how, very young, to hide well and to sleep in places that were very uncomfortable—but were places that were my safe haven.

My dad not being able to touch me and do things that he wanted to do made him angry. So because of that I spent years and years the product of his abuse. I didn't understand how he could get away with beating me the way that he would beat me. Nobody would help me and I would cry and wonder "Why doesn't somebody stop this, don't you see what he is doing? Won't somebody help me, won't somebody do something?"

I vividly remember one night feeling as though I was just going to lie down and die. I wanted to die to keep from feeling the pain. My body was so sore from him having kicked me in my stomach and hitting me in the head. Then I remembered something that my grandfather said to me. I began to weep because I could feel his presence there as his words rang out in my despair. He had told me before he died that no matter what happened in my life that God would always be there with me; that I could go to a secret place and He would just rock me in His arms. His words gave me a place of refuge—even if only in my mind. I remember spending so many evenings in my secret place just feeling Jesus as He would rock me in His arms. In my time of trouble the Lord was my refuge and strength. I understand now that the enemy wanted me to think I had no future. He wanted me to think I was damaged goods because of what had happened to me. Luke 22:31-32, "And the Lord said, 'Simon, Simon! Indeed, Satan has asked for you, that he may sift you as wheat: But I have prayed for you, that your faith shall not fail; and when you have returned to me, strengthen your brethren."

Have no doubt, the devil hates you, and he desires to sift you. He wants to get you to give up, he wants to rob you of your innocence, rob you of your resources, rob you of your finances, rob you of your sanity, rob you of your marriage, rob you of your good reputation, and rob you of your joy. In fact, if he can kill you as a child all the better. And he uses whatever vessel that will make itself available to him. My earthly father didn't know he was being used to try to rob me of my future.

What had I done so bad to deserve to be beaten all the time? I recall being in the kitchen washing dishes and my father came in and took one of the glasses that I had washed, picked it up and said, "this glass is dirty, you can't do nothing right." He then took every dish out of the cabinet and had me wash every single dish in the kitchen. And when I finally finished, he took a plate and hit me over the head with it! Dazed I stumbled to my room and cried for hours.

Why was this happening to me? I was not an only child, why was I the center of his abuse? Was it because I didn't want him to touch me? I spent years even after being married feeling dirty when having sex (didn't understand making love) when it should have been a beautiful experience. I pretended I was getting something out of the touches that made my mind silently scream. Feeling if I didn't want sex I wasn't normal. I didn't want to be any more different that I already felt.

I wanted to hate my father so badly. I felt he didn't deserve my love. Maybe you have had those same feelings about someone who has hurt you. Perhaps you couldn't do anything about it then but that was then and this is now. I beg you don't spend as many years as I did wishing things were different. Don't empower your past experiences. As a matter of fact, decide that you will not be robbed one more day of "wholeness." You have the authority to take back your life! The Bible says in Luke 10:19 "Behold, I give you the authority to trample on serpents and scorpions, and over all the power of the enemy, and nothing shall by any means hurt you." Don't waste time being pitiful when you can be powerful! You need to trust that the King of kings and the Lord of lords and the Father of all resources will provide your every need.

The New International version of Luke 22: 1-6 says, "Now the Feast of Unleavened Bread drew near, which is called Passover. And the chief priests and the scribes sought how they might kill Him, for they feared the people. Then Satan entered Judas, surnamed Iscariot, who was numbered one of the twelve. So he went his way and conferred with the chief priests and captains, how he might betray Him to them. And they were glad, and agreed to give him money. So he promised and sought opportunity to betray Him to them in the absence of the multitude."

You may think that the enemy will roll over and play dead but he will not. Satan is going to continue to watch you and wait as he did with Judas, for you to make a mistake and if he can, he will manipulate you. Don't underestimate the enemy just because you survived one temptation. That booger is coming again and again. Why? Because he has seen a glimpse of your future and he doesn't want you to get to it. You can stay angry until it motivates every action of your life. You can become captive for so long until you don't know what it feels like to be free. I was in prison and didn't even realize it. And it all started as I began nursing my shame and my anger. I played it back over and over in my mind.

I had let my feeling plant seeds of disdain for my father. The Word of God says in Galatians 6:7, "Do not be deceived, God is not mocked; for whatever a man sows, that he will also reap." We reap what we sow. Even if we feel justified for sowing it. It is a spiritual principal. My thoughts were so filled with hatred; I could not give or receive love. I became the product of my thought life, thoughts that produced sickness and hindered healing. This truth was revealed to me when my health was attacked. Unknowingly I had given my father so much power over me that I was feeling the results in my poor health. I needed to let go and didn't know how.

If you have made mistakes, there is always another chance for you. You may have a fresh start any moment you choose, for this thing we call 'failure' is not the falling down, but the staying down. – Mary Pickford

CHAPTER THREE

News from Home

Chapter Three

News from Home

I walked out to the middle of the stage and began my monologue. The audience began to laugh at me, but I kept going. Soon I realized there was silence. I was captivating them. They could feel the pain of my character Juanita. As the emotions of this character went from her crying to her being angry then laughing, the audience was right there with her as she talked about her wanting to be pregnant and the injustice of the time. As the character reached a crescendo she fell to the floor. The audience got on their feet giving a standing ovation!

College was the best time of my life. I was running for "Miss Student Union," and it was time for all the contestants to present their talents. While most of the other ladies sung or danced, I dared to be different and presented a monologue from, "Blues for Mr. Charlie" As I watched the audience applause I had no doubt, I had given the performance of my life. My heart pounded as they read the tally. Third place, then second place and then finally, first place! Did they say my name! I looked down at Robert as tears of joy ran down my face. His smile affirmed me that it was real. I was crowned the College's "Miss Student Union".

Robert was my first real boyfriend. He felt more like a friend. There was something about him that made me feel safe and Lord knows given my background I needed to feel safe. I had been able to share so much with him. His listening to me and his always reassuring me gave me hope that there was a real chance at feeling some normalcy in my life. In fact, for the first time I knew what it felt like to have male affection and attention that was not perverted. I finally knew what love was supposed to feel like. We even had our own planet which we named Noxzema. We had discovered it while riding in a canoe looking up at the sky.

After the contest he walked me back to my dorm room. I was feeling on top of the world I was crowned queen and my king was standing beside me. Nothing would spoil this night for me. So I thought. As we entered the lobby of Diamond Hall, the house mother told Robert she needed to talk with him a minute. I thought that was rather strange. What was going on? Robert came over to me and said, "Let's take a walk." I told him it was almost curfew I couldn't go anywhere. The house mother reassured me it was alright. Now I knew something was up. We walked outside and stood under a large oak tree as he took my hand. "What's wrong?" He told me that they had just gotten news that my father had passed away. The strangest thing happened. I laughed. Then I cried uncontrollably. I don't think my mind knew how to process his death. Shortly after that I broke things off with Robert. To this day I don't know why. I loved him and for years could not see him without crying. For some reason I felt like I didn't deserve to be loved and happy and Robert made me feel both.

The most liberating thing in my life was when the Holy Spirit prompted me as I was reading a scripture in Mark 11:25-26 "And whenever you stand praying, if you have anything against anyone, forgive him and let it drop (leave it, let it go), in order that your Father, who is in heaven may forgive *you*. But if you do not forgive, neither will your father in heaven forgive your trespasses." I wanted to shout out, "But he doesn't deserve my forgiveness!" I thought I heard the Lord say, "Forgive him for *you* not for him." I began to cry as a peace came over me and I said, "I forgive you Daddy." It has been said when you forgive someone you release a prisoner and that prisoner is you. I thought his funeral had brought closure for me, but my mind still wanted to process the pain.

Be careful what you think on. My thoughts had consumed my life and held me captive from the life that God wanted and had divinely planned for me. I was allowing the enemy to alter my destiny. After my father had passed away, he was still controlling my life from the grave. I had to learn how to let go. I could only do that by changing my thought life. The Word of God says in Philippians 4:8 "Finally, brethren, whatever things are true, whatever things are noble, whatever things are just, whatever things are pure, whatever things are lovely, whatever things are of good report, if there is any virtue and if there is anything praiseworthy, meditate on these things."

Further, it states in 2nd Corinthians 10:5, "Casting down arguments and every high thing that exalts itself against the knowledge of God, bringing every thought into captivity to the obedience of Christ." Don't hold on to anything that does not exalt God. That's why there are so many people who wonder how their lives got so out of control. It began with wrong thinking.

The enemy uses your mind and your thoughts as his battleground, and he never comes in a blatant way where you can say, "Oh, there's the devil." No, he always comes incognito. He camouflages himself. Remember in Mat. 16:22 when Peter rebuked Jesus? It says, "Then Peter took him aside and began to rebuke him, saying, far be it from you, Lord; this shall not happen to you!" Peter didn't have a clue what was going on, but Jesus knew the wrong thought had been planted in Peter's mind, so he spoke to that spirit speaking to Peter's mind. And said, "Get thee behind me, Satan: thou art an offence unto me." So be careful whose voice you are listening to. If it isn't the voice of God, reject it.

The enemy of your soul wants you to feel like you deserve bad things happening to you. He is a liar! Reject such thoughts. The Word of God says in John 10:4, "And when he brings out his own sheep, he goes before them; and the sheep follow him, for they know his voice."

If you are being told that the reason you are being beaten is because you deserve it, that is not the voice of God. Reject that thought! Or if you have been told that a man doesn't love you unless he hits you—please reject that thought! Or if you have been told that your birth was a mistake and that you will never amount to anything, send that thought back to Hell. If you are being told that you don't have that ministry because you are too young or too old, reject that thought! Perhaps you have been told your past mistakes make you unfit for the Ministry. The Devil is a liar. Someone needs your testimony. And ladies, if you are being told that any man is better than no man. Send that thought of low self worth straight to hell!

Perhaps, you've been told you don't have a husband yet because you don't deserve love. Reject that thought! If you are being told that you don't have the house you want because God is holding out on you, don't receive that thought. Wrong thinking! If you are being told that you are sick because God is trying to teach you something, don't receive that thought. If it doesn't line up with the Word of God, it is a lie. God said, "I know what you have need of before you even ask." In Psalms 84:11 He says, "No good thing will He withhold from those who walk uprightly."

It's time to walk out in your God given calling. The devil does not want you to know the value of what is on the inside of you. The Bible says in Ephesians 3: 20, "Now to him who is able to do exceedingly abundantly above all that we ask or think, according to the power that works in us" It's in you! You need to have confidence in what is in you. The greatest wealth in the world is in Africa and yet there are people dying and suffering from lack. People are walking in taking their stuff because they don't know the value of what they have.

It is okay to recognize what you do well. You don't have to wait for someone else to acknowledge your talents and gifts. You don't need someone to solidify you. God has justified you. I wasted years of my life needing affirmation from others. It came out of my need to be accepted. You need to know it is okay to be you. The life God has for you is larger than the life you are presently in. Your storms are an opportunity to allow what is on the inside of you to come out. It is not what you go through; it is how you go through it. The fact that you are still here lets you know you are a survivor. No matter what the enemy tries, be encouraged! Jesus has your back!!!! Jesus has already prayed that your faith will not fail.

It's not what you gather,

but what you scatter that

tells what kind of life you

have lived!

CHAPTER FOUR

A Mother's Love

Chapter Four

A Mother's Love

"Before I formed thee in the belly I knew thee; and before thou camest forth out of the womb I sanctified thee, and I ordained thee a prophet unto the nations." Jeremiah 1:5. It was not until after my father passed, that I could see the real beauty of my mother. I know things had not been easy for her, but she had a heart bigger than most. She possessed a loving and giving spirit. Mother was always taking someone in and if not that she was feeding the whole neighborhood. You could always go there and get something to eat. She was the neighborhood mom. She was very unselfish when it came to her kids needs. She was the type of person if there were only four pieces of pie and four kids she would pretend she didn't like that kind of pie anyway, so we should eat it. I never recall being without the things we needed. I wish my mother had lived long enough to enjoy her life to the fullest but she passed away the week she was to retire from work.

I just want to take a moment and bless moms. A woman has been given a unique gift. It is one that could not be any closer to God, the gift to recreate, the gift of being a mother. Motherhood is the highest calling. Inside of the mother has been placed a nurturing and loving heart. God has entrusted you with a life. I don't think anything impacts a child's life like a mother. God has a perfect plan for the life of every child and how that mother responds to that plan helps in the development of who that child is to become. You have an obligation to seek God on behalf of your children so you can guide their lives. You have to know when to teach and train and you have to know when to let go.

Ask God to help you to see the potential in your child. Remind them that they can become whatever they are willing to put their mind and heart to. They need to know that they don't have to be like anyone else because they are perfect for that which God has designed them. So many kids are mimicking their friends trying to fit in. Wouldn't it be something if we taught them how to be leaders and not followers? They need to know you believe in them. Speak confidence into your children. When they know you have confidence in them, it helps them have confidence in themselves. Let them know they are important to you. Get involved in the things they care about. Give them daily hugs and remind them they are loved.

Single Moms stop holding your children responsible for decisions you and their father have made. Every child is a gift from God. No child is a mistake. If you have been blessed with a child know that God has entrusted you with an awesome opportunity to pour your love into another human being and in return you will get the love you need. Most important you need to pray for your children. You can pray them out of the gangs. Pray them off drugs. Pray for a role model into their lives. Fight for your children! Live a life before them that you will want them to eminent. You can't give to them what you yourself don't possess. God has given you the authority to speak into the lives of your children. Pray over your children.

Please don't allow the enemy to put you on a guilt trip about what you have not done in the past. We all have missed the mark at times. After all we were once children ourselves and our emotions are responding to our own childhoods. Often we are covering our own dysfunctional upbringing. However, you don't have to pass that on to your children. You can start now changing things for them. You can start by asking God to heal you so you don't pour that same pain into their lives. If there has been walls between you and your children God will restore your relationship with them as you turn to Him trusting in His love. No one else can be what you can be for your children. There is a reason God chose you to be their mother. There is something in you they need.

It is so important that we give our children the nurturing and love they need as a child. When they don't get this their inner child will go into adulthood with feelings of inadequacy. They may never feel "good enough." It will be easier for others to control them because they have no confidence in themselves or they are so needy they will settle for anything. They may find themselves trying to live up to others expectations and never finding their own true identity. You can make a difference. Let God release you so you can release them.

A Mother's Prayer

Father God,

I speak into the lives of every mother reading these pages, that in the Name of Jesus; they will receive the healing they need in their lives. As they experience your touch, they will be able to pour peace, confidence, acceptance and love back into the lives of their children.

I pray for them the courage to hold on in difficult times understanding that you will never leave them or forsake them. I come in agreement with your Word that no weapon formed against them shall prosper. I come in agreement with each mother that their children are loosed from every demonic spirit of oppression, procession and distraction from their purpose. In the Name of Jesus, I pray that they are free to become that for which you have ordained.

Father help them to rely on your strength when they feel they themselves have none left.

When they are lonely and need to be touched, let your love embrace them. Never let them forget that their lives matter. I ask it all in the Name of Jesus. Amen

A diamond is merely a lump of coal that did well under pressure. – Author Unknown

CHAPTER FOUR

The God Kind of Love

Chapter Four

The God Kind of Love

I grew up watching Leave it to Beaver, The Donna Reed Show, The Andy Griffith Show, and Father Knows Best. They were television programs that taught me what family life was supposed to be like. There was always a pie baking in the oven and every family crisis had a happy ending. It is strange how we will make something else our reality when our own truth doesn't measure up. By now you realize that I grew up in a "dysfunctional home." Although the experience was painful, God is teaching me everyday how to allow Him to turn what the enemy meant for harm into my good.

It is a process to release your pain and disappointments. But it is one we must go through in order to heal. Because I didn't understand that then, many times I felt all alone. As a child I wondered if I was being punished because I was a bad girl. As I grew older praying to the God of my grandfather, who had become my God, I'd wonder where he was when I was going through tough times and at times wondered if He was angry with me too.

I have since learned that the enemy was doing all he could to pull down my faith in God's ability in my life. He didn't want me to live to tell the story. It was Satan's test not God's. My Heavenly Father knew what I was made out of, even when I didn't; so during the test the teacher didn't talk. That is when he watched me as I had to rely on all the principals I have been taught. It is during these times that we find out who we really are. Even though God doesn't bring despair into our lives we can rest assured according to 1st Cor. 10:13, "No temptation has overtaken you except such as is common to man; but God is faithful, who will not allow you to be tempted beyond what you are able, but with the temptation will also make the way to escape, that you may be able to bear it." There is not a doubt in my mind I am a survivor because God is with me. He protected me when I could not protect myself. He taught me that there is a Power greater than myself inside me. You have the "Power" of the "Holy Spirit" inside you.

Don't give in or give up! You can make it! Look within and draw from the well which will never run dry.

Abuse leaves you broken. I have had to deal with all the insecurities I had about my own self worth. I didn't think I deserved a healthy relationship so parts of me were left in unfulfilled relationships. My first marriage was abusive and destructive. I couldn't understand what it was in me that would cause me to go from an abusive father to an abusive husband. If you are not careful the dysfunction not dealt with in your childhood will follow you into your adult life. You will think that is how it is always going to be. I just wanted someone to love me. The problem was however, I didn't know what love felt like.

We find "dysfunctional families" all throughout the Bible. Some of these families are not much different from our own. We find examples from the Old Testament to the New Testament. The jealousy of Adam's son Cain motivated him to murder his brother Abel (Gen. 4:8). Noah got drunk (Gen. 9:21). So did Lot, and as a result, his daughters committed incest with him (Gen. 19:30-38).

Jacob's two wives bartered with each other for the right to sleep with him at night (Gen. 30:14-16). Jacob followed his parent's example of favoritism, and caused his own children to hate their brother Joseph, who they later sold into slavery (Gen. 37:3-28).

David, a man after God's own heart, committed adultery and murder. (2 Sam. 12:9-12) Because of this, his family disintegrated in a tragic sequence of events that included rape, incest, and murder. Even Jesus was ridiculed by His brothers and called mad by His extended family. (Mark3:21).

Regardless, if your story is like one in the Bible or completely different, we all have issues. Every family has its secrets that they need to get real about. Stop the cover up and expose the enemy and let's all meet at the foot of the cross. It is there where God meets us and works out His purpose in us. He uses our "mess" and transforms it into a "message."

Growing up in a dysfunctional family, makes you feel different from other children. The sad thing is when a child is not parented they aren't prepared for adulthood. There are so many adults with a little child inside them still needing to be nurtured and loved so a healthy development can take place. Broken children make broken adults.

Broken adults deal with their pains in different ways. Some through meaningless sex, some through the use of alcohol as my father did or drugs and whatever else you may think will help you forget. Still others are in denial and suffer depression. And for those who cannot deaden the pain from their past, they seek to impose it on others. This often shows up in the form of rape, murder or beating their spouse or children. I have known people to even mutilate their own bodies.

I have opened myself up because there are those who have lived what I have lived. There are still those who still feel the sting of the past. There are those who want to let go and live a normal life, but aren't sure what normal is. I know your pain! But this I know even more, there is help. Jesus came to set the captive free. He wants to wash you and turn your mourning into laughter. He wants to hold you and rock you in His arms as He has me so many times. Just as real as your pain is, so is the love of Abba Father. It is time to let the pain go so you can meet Jesus at the cross. Realize that everyday you hold on to what has happened in the past you are giving it power over you. You have the greatest weapon to fight a painful past, it is called forgiveness. You may ask, "How can I forgive someone who molested me, or raped me?"

How do I forgive hurt that has consumed me so long? Or I didn't deserve what happened to me." No, you did not. But neither do they deserve another day of consuming your thoughts or your life. Let them go so you can be free.

Child of God, we were never promised we would not have trying times. But look at what the Word of God does say in Isaiah 43:1. "But now, this is what the Lord says, he who created you, O Jacob, he who formed you, O Israel: "Fear not, for I have redeemed you; I have summoned you by name; you are mine. When you pass through the waters, I will be with you; and when you pass through the rivers, they will not sweep over you. When you walk through the fire, you will not be burned; the flames will not set you ablaze." God promises to be there in the midst of our troubles. God says, "The path you must take may be through the rivers, but you will not drown; the path may be through the fire, but you will not be consumed in the flames." He knows each of us by name. He knows the number of hairs on each of our heads. There is nothing that can happen in our lives that is too big for God to handle. That includes my abuse.

All of us have a deep need to love and be loved. Despite my scars, I still loved my parents. I know exactly what kind of home I lived in. I know

41

that my father was an alcoholic, who was physically and verbally abusive. I know that my mother felt helpless in the situation. These things did not stop me from loving my parents and wanting their acceptance. So much so, that I was an over achiever at school. I wanted them to be proud of me. But nothing I accomplished seemed to be good enough. I won awards and contest at school, but there were no family members there to see me receive them. I am thankful for one of my teachers that always made sure I got to where I was to be. And an Aunt that encouraged me. I still loved my family even though no one showed up.

As have others who grew up in a dysfunctional home, I have had to come to terms with the anger and deep disappointment that result from parental abuse and neglect. But it was Christ's acceptance of me that enabled me to accept and love them. Jesus gave us unconditional love and God so loved us that He gave Jesus. Our Heavenly Father loves us unconditionally. Romans 5: 6-8 says, "For when we were still without strength, in due time Christ died for the ungodly. For scarcely for a righteous man will one die; yet perhaps for a good man someone would even dare to die. But God demonstrates His own love toward us, in that while we were still sinners, Christ died for us." These verses use the words "powerless," "ungodly," and "sinners" to describe us. Christ died for people who didn't have it all together. That certainly fits me because I was anything but together.

God's love is based only on his mercy. I have been let down many times but, I don't have to look over my shoulder all the time, wondering if God is going to let me down or walk out on me because I blew it. I don't have to worry that God might change his mind about me because I am not meeting certain expectations. God already knows the worst about me and he chose to love me! And for me that is saying a lot! And just as Father God loves us unconditionally, I have received that same love from my children.

Just as I love them despite their performance they have loved me despite mine. My children do not love me because I try hard to be the kind of parent I would like to have had. They love me because I am their mother. When I fall short, they do not love me any less. They love me because they are my children. What is more, I love them in the same way. I do not love them because they try to do what pleases me. But I loved them while they were yet in my belly and if they break my heart in the future, I know that I will love them still. I love them because they are my children. And God loves us because we are his. God has a plan for each of us. The Bible says in Jeremiah 29:11, "For I know the thoughts that I think toward you, saith the Lord, thoughts of peace, and not of evil, to give you an expected end." You may not know where you are headed, but God does. And 1st Corinthians 2:9 tells us, "Eye has not seen, nor ear heard, nor have entered into the heart of man, the things which God has prepared for those who love him." God has broken the spirit of "not being good enough" from over my life and I pray now in the Name of Jesus, that it is broken from over your life as well.

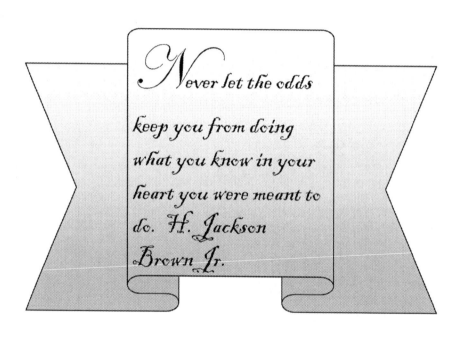

Never let the odds keep you from doing what you know in your heart you were meant to do. H. Jackson Brown Jr.

CHAPTER FIVE

Restored In Him

Chapter Five

Restored In Him

Romans 8:18,
> "For I consider that the sufferings of this present time are not worthy to be compared with the glory which shall be revealed in us."

I love garage sales. I bought this old antique vase once for fifty cents. It had screws, nails and other odds and ends stored in it. It was being used for a purpose other than what it had been designed for. It was really cruddy looking. But you can't always tell what's under a thing. Looks can be deceiving. Even though it didn't look like much at first, it was beautiful after I cleaned it up and took out all the junk that had been stored in it.

A friend talked me into taking it to an antique shop to see what they would give me for it. I did, and after some deliberation, was offered two hundred and fifty dollars. I decided not to sell. I felt if they were willing to give me that much; it was obviously worth a lot more.

Unlike that vase, we were fashioned by the Hands of God. We were made in His image. No wonder he doesn't want to sell us out to the Devil. We are worth more to him than we can imagine. When we are cleansed by His Blood it restores us. He takes out of us what is not supposed to be in us, so we can return to our original purpose.

When we find ourselves in relationships out side of marriage, we are putting things in us that hinder our original purpose. You lose sight of your purpose when all kinds of things are dumped in you. You were not designed for someone else's garbage.

Often we won't allow ourselves to be cleansed because we are stuck somewhere in the past, feeling we don't deserve to be washed. Besides, washing off the façade would expose the real you. Believe it or not, the real you is not who you think. It is not your shame but rather His glory.

Be encouraged and do not allow the pain of the past to poison your future. We all have had challenges. We fall down but we can get up. Praise God for new mercies every morning. It is time we stop telling people how big our problems are and tell them how big our God is. We all have issues to deal with. However, when we replace our shame with honesty we uncover the enemy. He can only hide in the dark places of our lives.

Uncovering ourselves allows the light of the Holy Spirit to shine into our dark places. In His light is hope and purpose. Don't ever let anyone else assign you your purpose or allow anyone to plug anything in you that will cause you to short circuit.

Because I had been hurt and victimized, I became so eager to please. The reason for this was because I wanted to be loved. This is when it is easy to allow others to use us for their purpose and before you realize it, you are trying to become someone they want and lose yourself in the process.

You need to know it is alright to be you. Once you discover who you are, I am sure you will find beauty instead of ashes. What is it that you have wanted to do with your life and because of fear or what others thought you put it on hold? Find it and act on it!

What is the worst thing that can happen if you walk out your own God given purpose? You mess up? So what? God has a mop and He can clean it up. God will never call you to what He doesn't qualify you to. And where He leads His provision follows. When we empty ourselves of everyone else's plan for our lives we can be open to hear God's.

I once heard a story of a young man who was seeking God. So he went to a well known and wise sage for help and asked how he could find God? Well, the old sage told him to go with him to a river that was nearby. They walked until the water got up to their chins. Then the old man took the young man by his neck and pushed him under water until he almost drowned. He finally let the young man up and they found their way back to the bank of the river. The young man said to the old man, "You almost killed me. What did that have to do with finding God?" The old man asked him, "While you were under the water, what did you want more than anything else?" The young man said, "Air." The old man replied, "When you want God as much as much as you wanted air, you will find Him." Jeremiah 29:13 says, "And you will seek me and find me, when you search for me with all your heart."

When you have had so much messed up in your life along with a broken heart and relationships, you may feel you don't have enough strength to run on. You may be dealing with anger or hurt. If you have not experienced the pain that someone is going through, it is easy to tell them to "just get over it." Jesus understands this. We see His heart for hurting messed up people in His Word. When we don't have the strength to move forward, Jesus meets us where we are. In John 4:6-18 Jesus met the Samaritan Woman at the well of her hurt and misery.

"Now Jacob's well was there. Jesus therefore, being wearied with his journey, sat thus by the well: it was about the sixth hour. A woman from Samaria came to draw water: Jesus said to her, "Give me a drink". For his disciples had gone away into the city to buy food. Then the woman of Samaria said to him, "How is it that you, being a Jew, ask a drink from me, a Samaritan woman?" For Jews have no dealings with Samaritans." Jesus answered and said to her, "If you knew the gift of God, and who it is who says to you, 'Give me a drink,' you would have asked him, and he would have given you living water." The woman said to him, "Sir, you have nothing to draw with, and the well is deep. Where then do you get that living water? Are you greater than our father Jacob, who gave us the well, and drank from it himself, as well as his sons and his livestock?" Jesus answered and said to her, "Whoever drinks of this water will thirst again, but whoever drinks of the water that I shall give him will never thirst. But the water that I shall give him will become in him a fountain of water springing up into everlasting life." The woman said to him, "Sir, give me this water, that I may not thirst, nor come here to draw." Jesus said to her, "Go, call your husband, and come here." The woman answered and said, "I have no husband."

Jesus said to her, "you have well said, 'I have no husband,' For you have had five husbands, and the one whom you now have is not your husband; in that you spoke truly."

Jesus knew the void in her life that five husbands, and now a sixth man she was living with, couldn't fill. He knew how she felt and that her life was full of nothing but bitterness, shame and turmoil. Have you ever felt like there was nothing left to live for? Have you ever felt that your life was worthless and meaningless? That even **you** were ashamed of **you**? She didn't know that she could not do anything bad enough that God would not still love her. She didn't know that he loved her so much that he was there that day just for her. Wow! Can you imagine Jesus stopping by just to meet your need?

Jesus doesn't look at tradition. He loves us all exactly where we are in our lives. It doesn't matter what your background looks like, or what others think of you. 1 Corinthians 15:3 says, "While we were yet sinners Christ died for us." He loves us all, even though we don't deserve it. He looks at each and every one of us with love and acceptance in His eyes and His heart, even those of us that society over looks or looks down upon. She had never experienced that kind of love. She had no idea what that kind of love felt like.

She did know what it felt like to have people gossiping about her. It's even worse when the gossip is true. She did not want other women whispering about her. If you have ever been in a barber shop or a hair salon, you can relate. That's why this woman went at the hottest time of the day when no one else would be there. Hauling water was hard work, no one wanted to do it in the heat. That's why everyone else did it in the cool of the day. But this woman went at a time when she knew she didn't have to face the other women. The heat was more pleasant than their glances and comments. She knew what type of life she lived. Jesus knew the heart of this woman which no one else could see. He knew that something needed to change for her.

Have you ever felt so dirty that you believed that you couldn't stand in the presence of God? She must have felt this way because she asked Jesus *"How is it that you, being a Jew, ask a drink from me, a Samaritan woman? for Jews have no dealings with Samaritans."* God knew her shame and her deepest secrets but He's not waiting to condemn her but rather to release her. She was soon to find out that He had come to bring healing and restoration to her. He came to offer her "Living Water."

This woman is no stranger to thirst. She just didn't know what she was thirty for. She was at the well to draw water. She has been divorced five times and is living with a man when that was not her husband, when she meets Jesus. How many relationships have you been in because you were thirsty for a lasting, durable and stable relationship? Have you slept with someone and felt dirty and wondered why you were there in the first place? Maybe it was just because you just wanted to feel something, anything but dead inside! What you may not realize is that you are thirsty for God. Psalms 42:1,2 says;

"As the deer pants for the water brooks, so pants my soul for you,
O God. My soul thirsts for God, for the living God.
When shall I come and appear before God?"

That same Living Water is ours today. It will fill you and satisfy you no matter how deep the wound; it will wash away the pain. The Word of God says in Matthew 11:28, "Come to me all you who labor and are heavy laden, and I will give you rest."

Are you tired of going from one bad relationship to another? Are you sick of not being able to get high enough, long enough? Are you tired of having one man after another touch you? Are you tired of washing yourself and still feeling dirty? What is it that you are using to satisfy your thirst? I invite you to drink of the well that will never run dry. I invite you to allow this Living Water to flow over every dead part in you and awaken the life within you, that you may once again flourish and be all that God has called you to be.

Instead of being desperate, be delivered. Just like the Samaritan woman had to make a choice, you can chose, that this is the day that will mark the beginning of the first day of the rest of your life.

Deut 30:19:
". . . I have set before you life and death, blessing and cursing;
therefore choose life, that both you and your descendants may
live; that both you and your descendants may live; . . ."

Choose Life!!!!! All that has tried to hurt you in the past is a lie. The truth is that you are more than a conqueror in Christ Jesus. The truth is that no weapon formed against you can prosper. The truth is greater is He that is in you than he that is in the world. The truth is that you are not just an heir but a joint heir with Christ! The truth is that you are the King's kid!

So take off the sackcloth and ashes and allow the Father to put on you the robe of righteousness. Put the book down and shout out to yourself that, "I am somebody! I have over come by the blood of the lamb and the word of my testimony! I am free and who the Son has set free is free indeed!"

This is my prayer for you that you would never go back to that dark place again but instead that you will drink from the Living Water that is Christ Jesus. If God can do it for me, he will do it for you because he is no respecter of persons.

The problem is thinking you don't deserve any better. It is like a dog going back to his vomit. Insanity has been described as doing the same thing over and over and expecting the result to be different. We have to be careful of familiar spirits. It is just like my having gone from an abusive father to an abusive husband. Imagine the slave master releasing the slave and he has the freedom to do what he wants and instead he goes back and works for the slave master again. He doesn't know there is a different life awaiting him.

Jesus has freed us from the slave master but we keep going back to him anyway. If you've been told over and over again that this is all that you are worth, you will soon believe it. We have to spiritually reprogram ourselves so instead of thinking the way the World says, we think the way the Word says.

We do this by putting more of the Word in us. Our reality must not be the world but the Word. Whose truth do I choose? Actually, it is no contest because the only real truth lays in His Word. I can never be free until I first see myself free and I can never see myself free until I believe that I have a right to be free. I have to trust that God's Word is true and stand on that truth.

Be aware of familiar spirits which can be a chain that keeps you tied to your past. We need to think about the victory that we have in Him through the Word. If that becomes more powerful than the pain that binds you then those chains have to break loose!

You have to take possession of your future. The Bible says "The Kingdom of heaven suffers violence and the violent take it by force." This new—found freedom only comes if you take it! You have to choose it and take it. The day for being passive is over. Aggressively possess what you have every right to according to His Word and DON'T SETTLE FOR ANYTHING LESS!

Father God,

I plead the blood of Jesus over this person. I pray that the word of life that you spoke of in your word would come and remind this person of the life that you have so freely given. I pray that the darkness in this person's life would be revealed and removed by the light! I pray a hedge of protection around him or her. I pray that you set angels round about them. I pray that you will be their refuge and their strength in time of trouble. That no accident will overtake them and no calamities will come near them. I pray that you would prosper them and that he/she will be in good health even as their soul prospers. I pray peace into their lives and that their sorrow is replaced with joy. In the Name of Jesus, Amen.

Don't wait for something big to occur.

Start where you are, with what you have, and that will always lead you into something greater.
– Mary Manin Morrissey

CHAPTER SIX

You Are Never Alone

Chapter Six

You Are Never Alone

My feet were hurting and my heart pounding because I knew I had to hurry and get back to my kids. I had been left in a strange city with forty dollars in my pocket and was staying with my three children in a twenty-dollar-a-night room. This is how my first husband had left us. I knew I had to find work, my children needed to eat and I had to keep a roof over their heads. Early that morning, I had locked the door of the room and explained to my oldest child how I had to go and find work so we could have a place to live and I needed her to be a really big girl and look after her sisters. She listened to all the rules and how she was not to open the door for anyone. Trying to be brave she said, "Ok, Mom don't worry." But I knew she was afraid. I prayed as I left there for God to please look after my girls, because I was more than a little worried. I had no choice, I couldn't take three children job hunting.

After hours of searching I was hired by a flower shop and could start the next morning. Tired and frustrated, I sat on the bench at the bus stop and cried while asking, "Lord, how am I going to do this? I can't leave the kids alone everyday. My poor babies deserve so much better than this." As I sat there crying, I could sense someone had come and sat next to me. I looked up and it was an older lady wearing a hat and white gloves. "Sweetheart," she said, "I don't know what is happening with you, but God wanted me to tell you, it was going to be alright." I began to cry even more as I was telling this complete stranger all I was going through. She patted my hand and said, "My car is close by. Let's go get your children. You are coming home with me."

As I look back on this, she could have been anyone. I didn't know why I would trust a complete stranger; but I felt a peace that it was alright. She kept my kids during the day while I worked and we stayed there until I had enough money saved for a place of our own. I went back a few weeks later to once again thank her for what she had done for us, but strangely, she had moved. I don't know where she went, but I will never forget that special angel.

I can see so many times in my life when I have felt all alone and in each instance I can now see God's hand. He has never left me alone. There was a time there was no food in the house and I put on a pot of boiling water and put plates on the table. I called the kids to come so we could prepare to eat. They listened as I prayed and thanked God for our food. I heard one of the children say, "Mom, has really lost it. There is no food." Before I could finish praying there was a knock at the door and it was a couple from the Church. They said they had sat down to eat and the Lord told them to pack it all up and bring it to us. God was teaching my children how he honors faith and at the same time teaching me something about sowing.

I believe that was a result of previous seeds sown. Not long before that incident, at Christmas time the Lord had impressed up on me instead of buying the children toys to give them an even more valuable gift. I told them we were going to take the money we would have spent and cook meals for the homeless and make them goodie bags. The kids helped me pass them out and saw first hand how thankful they were for the little. I don't think it bothered them at all that I hadn't bought them toys. To this day, even as adults they are still sensitive to the needs of others.

About six months or so later, I went back to the area where we had fed so many and there were people there who still remembered us. Since that time the Lord enabled us to work with a local supermarket setting up food banks for the local needy. When you have been hungry you can appreciate his provision in a different light. I have learned to live by the motto, "you only look down when you are helping someone else up."

Sometimes life throws you a curve ball, that's why when you have Jesus Christ you can keep coming up to bat. Trust him even when there are strikes against you, because he will come up to bat for you as the pinch hitter. Never quit because Jesus will not quit on you. I could have made excuses for myself. I had been molested, abused and abandoned. What would that gotten me, sympathy? That doesn't feed kids or put a roof over your head. My children trusted me to provide for them. I trusted God to provide for us all. Besides lack is a curse not a blessing. If we don't know what we should have, how are we going to know that we should get up and go get it? I knew if one door was shut another had to be opened. I had seen it too many times, not to believe.

Soon afterwards, I got a job selling cars and things changed financially very quickly for us. I really had the favor of God as the commissions rolled in. For several months I was top salesperson. I was given a demo which meant I had a new car to drive without a payment. Isn't that just like our Father to make us the head and not the tail?

I was able to get a nice place for us to live and nice things for the kids. I remembered what the minister had said at our church when teaching on tithing. He had suggested that instead of tithing ten percent which was our obligation to the Lord that we tithe where we wanted to be instead of where we were. In other words if I made three hundred dollars and gave thirty, that is required of me and I would be blessed for my obedience. But if I made three hundred and tithe fifty I would be giving in faith to my future increase. Every week I would give more than ten percent and an offering and each month I saw substantial increase. That principal changed our lives. God truly is the Lord of multiplication, but you must give him something to multiply.

I can honestly say I have seen the favor of God on my life. And I can also honestly say it took my growing up to recognize it. It is settled in my spirit that God loves me and He wants His best for me. So much so He will meet my need wherever I am. Thank God, with all the things my daughters went through they are still all educated professional women, who know the Lord.

That is the love of the Father. I am thankful he also sent "Mr. Right" into my life after so many hurts by men. He is a man rooted in the Word of God. Coming into a blended family had its challenges as well, but that is a story for another time.

Know that all of us have battles we have fought or those in which we now fight. I don't know what yours is, but this I know, you are not alone. There is no sickness He has not already healed. There is no abuse He cannot sooth. There is no shame He cannot cleanse.

I can give you reasons to give up but I rather give you reasons to move forward to God's plan for your life. You were not a mistake; you were born for a purpose and with purpose. You are necessary. You are valuable. No one else on earth can do what you were designed to do. You are important to His total plan whether you realize it or not.

Let me share one other thing with you that the enemy uses to try to stop the plans God has for your life. He attacks your body. This is in the hope that it will give you an affirmation that you don't deserve a good life. He wants you to believe that God has put something on you. He is a Liar! Think about this, if you believe it is God's will for you to be sick why waste your time and go to Doctors? You would be walking in disobedience if he wanted you sick to teach you something and you were trying to get well. That is not our God! He wants us well. I recall when sickness attacked my body and I was in so much pain I had to literally crawl to the bathroom. There was a part of me that just wanted to lay on the floor and give up. I had to talk to my body as I crawled and remind it that it was well and not sick.

There is a character in the Bible in John 5 that I have to imagine was feeling pretty helpless also. For years he had gone to the pool hoping that today was his day. The Bible says in John 5: 5-9 "Now a certain man was there, who had an infirmity thirty-eight years. When Jesus saw him lying there, and knew that he already had been in that condition a long time, He said to him, "Do you want to be made well?" The sick man answered him, "Sir, I have no man to put me into the pool when the water is stirred up; but while I am coming, another steps down before me." Jesus said to him, "Rise, take up your bed and walk." And immediately the man was made well, took up his bed and walked. And that day was the Sabbath."

Do you feel like you have been in the same place for a long time and nothing is changing? Do you feel like every time you try to get up someone is in the way and knocks you back down? This man had been going through the same thing for 38 years and the first thing that Jesus asked him is, "Will you be made whole?" You may think what a silly question. Of course he wants to be whole. He keeps showing up to get in the pool doesn't he? Showing up is not enough.

Jesus knew that the man needed to make a decision not excuses. He needed to make a decision to get up. We can blame everyone around us for our failure but the truth of the matter is we hold our own destiny in our hands. We can chose to blame our background, our race, our parents or the economy, but until we have made a decision that we are going to change the way we think, nothing else is going to change. Life may give us some tough breaks but it doesn't have to break us. I know making excuses is easier, but you can't afford them. They are too costly. They will cost you the quality of life that was meant for you. So what Jesus was asking was, "are you tired enough of your situation that you are ready to do something about it?" It is not until we release it all that we can receive what we need to move forward.

I encourage you find the strength in you to get up and move forward with an attitude that you will not wait for someone else to value you or promote you. You have so much inside you that is begging to be released. Rise up and walk! Stop crying over what you can't do a thing about. Focus! If one door is shut go through another. If you can't find the door then cut through the wall. Do something; don't just lay there!

There were many days I felt like giving up but the Word of God compelled me to keep getting up. When I was diagnosed with fibromyalgia and then Parkinson disease, I cried out, "Why is this happening to me?" Here I was prepared to move forward with engagements in place to do full time evangelizing and my body is severely attacked. Honestly, I was angry. I was moving forward in what I knew God had called me to, was I missing it somewhere? I went day after day not knowing what it felt like not to feel pain. I even questioned God. I wanted to know wasn't what I had gone through as a child enough? Why must I endure this too? I kept hearing Him say, "my grace is sufficient!" That was not what I wanted to hear. "Please God, come to my rescue!"

Once again, I remembered the foundation my grandfather had laid for me. I went back to the Word of God. I began to read over healing scriptures and repeat them daily. I told my body it would not accept anything less that what the Word says. If your body has been under attack here are some scriptures that really blessed me.

3 John 2
"Beloved, I pray that you may prosper in all things and be in health, just as your soul prospers."

Jeremiah 17:14
"Heal me, O LORD, and I shall be healed; Save me, and I shall be saved: for you are my praise."
NOTE—
Once a person finally understands that healing is a part of the finished work of grace along with salvation, paid for at the same time with the same healing Blood, then you can get excited about this verse saying; "You did it Lord for me!

> *Then according to this verse I will agree and say,* **I have healing just as I have salvation,** *it's mine NOW!"*

Psalm 34:19

> *"Many are the afflictions of the righteous, but the LORD delivers him out of them all." It's not that you won't have afflictions but you will not stay afflicted, just stand on His Word. It never fails!*

1 John 4:17

> *"Love has been perfected among us in this: that we may have boldness in the day of judgment; because as He is, so are we in this world."*

NOTE—Not only can we have boldness in the day of judgment, but we can have boldness now in this life, in the face of adversity, knowing who we are in Christ, knowing what belongs to us in Him and tenaciously holding onto it, refusing what the enemy wants us to have. As this verse says so clearly, as He is, so are we in this world. Think about that for a moment, how is He now? He is not sick, He is not diseased—it can't touch Him, and we are His body—the body of Christ. Insist on having the blessing of the Lord manifested in you—praise Him for it now, worship Him!!!

1 Corinthians 6:15-17

> *"Do you not know that your bodies are members of Christ? Shall I then take the members of Christ and make them members of a harlot? Certainly not! Or do you not know that he who is joined to a harlot is one body with her? For "the two," He says, "shall become one flesh." But he who is joined to the Lord is one spirit with Him."*

NOTE—I can't say it any clearer than this verse—we are one with Jesus Christ now. Sickness has no right to Him, so it has no legal right to us. It is illegal and off limits, it has no right to stay. Take a firm stand and run off the attack and the lies of the enemy. You belong to the Lord, you are washed in His precious Blood, the covenant Blood. Command sickness, disease to leave and insist on your covenant rights now, and don't quit until it changes and becomes just as the Word says it should be!!!

Daily I see changes in my health, because I have made a choice, I shall live and not die and declare the works of my God! My symptoms are not more powerful than His Word. Whose report do you believe? I believe the report of the Lord and by the stripes of Jesus I am healed! Thank God for His grace and the ministry inside me. I am glad He would not let me use my body as an excuse. I will continue to declare His Word.

What ever you are going through, stop feeling sorry for yourself. You don't need anyone to baby you. There comes a time even a baby stops pooping in his diaper. Oh, did I offend you? Then get mad enough to fight back. God has already won your victory; all you have to do is have the courage to show up on the battle field. You are worthy! So much so Christ laid his life down for you. Now it is time you lay down your bed and walk!

There is no logical reason why I am not crazy having been beaten in the head and even having a plate broken over my head by my father. I should be incapable of loving since I had only seen perverted love. I should have been academically challenged since I had so many emotional problems, but I was in the top percentile of my class in high school and college.

Heck, with all I've been through I should have been dead. But I'm not. What's the difference? JESUS! The devil should have killed me while I was a puppy but now I am a bull dog which knows who I am in Christ. I know how to fight back now.

It is never too late. You can't allow bad experiences to hold you back for the rest of your life. Satan is hoping that a painful past will keep you so distracted you won't be able to do what God has called you to do. Your future is too valuable to allow the devil to steal it from you. It is not God's will that you win a few and lose a few. God's will is that we triumph always. No matter how impossible your situation is, don't give up. Accept nothing short of your victory in Christ Jesus. Make your set backs a set up for a great victory.

Romans 3:4, "Indeed, let God be true, but every man a liar." Deception is Satan's mightiest weapon. Outside of deception he is helpless. If he can't deceive you, he can't defeat you, then he can't steal from you. Hosea 4:6 says, "My people are destroyed for lack of knowledge." If you don't know you have a right to issue the devil a restraining order, you will live in defeat. You can speak to him in the name of Jesus and command him to take his hands off you, your family, your neighborhood, your schools, your property and your future. He is supposed to be under your feet. That way he will not be able to control your mind.

Think about how powerful the Word of God is. There is so much power in His words that even if he said that the sky was purple from that moment forth it would be what God says it is. And He has given us the authority through the Name of Jesus, to speak to things that are not as though they were. Look at this, God is so great that when He swears He has to swear on Himself because there is none greater.

Our Maker, our Creator, the Creator of the universe can deliver us! In other words, God has our back! Know your rights because there is power in knowing who you are. You have the blood of Jesus running through your veins. You are a champion on the inside. So rise up in the power of His might. You are not a loser you are a winner. You are not a failure, you are a champion. You have unlimited potential. Speak to things that are not as though they were. Curse negative words that have been spoken over you, no matter who said them. You are what God says you are. See you through His eyes.

Finally after many years I understand what having a "Father" means. When I feel Father God's love it is not perverted but comforting. It is not conditional, but steadfast even when I'm not at my best. He may chastise me but never does He abuse me. He doesn't belittle me, but reassures me that I am a capable and worthy person. He is my protector. God is the perfect Parent. He heals the scars that have been caused by the mistakes of our earthly parents. He has not only made me free but set me back on course to be who God predestined me to be before I was born. I am enjoying the journey.

What the caterpillar calls the end of the world, the master calls a butterfly. – Richard Bach

CHAPTER SEVEN

That was Then, This is Now

Chapter Seven

That was Then, This is Now

**"I Can Do All Things Through Christ
Who Strengthens Me" Philippians 4:13**

How powerful this scripture is when we get a true revelation of its meaning. Let's rephrase it and see if it gets your attention, "Through Christ Who strengthens me, I can do all things." You are not talking about your own power, you are saying through Him! Without Him I am limited, but through Him there is nothing I can't do. What ever the need is in my life, I have the strength to wait on it because "His grace is sufficient." In Him we have strength we could not have any other way! He has given us the strength to be victors and not victims. If you're feeling defeated, it could be because you've been listening to the lies of the enemy. Satan is the father of lies. Refuse to listen to his accusations. "You shall know the truth and the truth shall set you free."

Our ability in Him is accessed by our faith. And faith has nothing to do with what you see. I couldn't see myself walking without excruciating pain. Everyday my body hurt in another place. My hand had tremors. I went a whole year without being able to sleep at night, but a couple of hours at a time, because I hurt so badly I wore socks everywhere I went. My feet were so swollen shoes wouldn't fit. I had over fifty prescriptions, as the doctors moved me from one medication to another, trying to find what would work. The problem was I would take one pill to stop something that was going on and it would cause something else and then another pill was needed to counteract the last. Have you ever been sick and tired of being sick and tired? Something had to change. It was not until I fought back with the Word of God that things began to turn around.

We have been given a covenant with God through the Blood of Jesus. The price has been paid for our sickness and diseases. We have been loosed from the bondage of the enemy and given authority to command sickness and disease to leave our body. We have authority in the Name of Jesus. However, authority is only good when you use it.

I had to speak to my body what the Word of God said. Day after day until my faith could see me running, could see me standing to take a shower alone, could see me able to button my clothes, I had to see me well. No matter what the symptoms said, I had to speak what the Word said, that I was not going to get well, I was already well, "by the stripes of Jesus." At the writing of this book, I am still speaking to symptoms and telling them they have no power over me; each day I am strengthened to move forward. Some who have seen the difference say I am a miracle, but I say I am a Believer!

I know that apart from Jesus, I can do nothing; but in Jesus I can do all things. I choose to see myself as He sees me according to His living Word. My life is hid with Christ in God. I must say the same things that God says in His Word. How can two walk together if they don't agree?

I choose to trust God during the process. His Word is the final authority in my life. My entire life must be based upon God and His living Word. Total surrender is my only choice. I am learning to meditate upon His Word day and night and follow as the Holy Spirit leads. As I place my confidence in Jesus, it is awesome to see how God steps into the circumstances of my life.

His ability in me, not only gives me strength in my physical body but my mind as well. I could never have the strength to leave the past behind had I not experienced God's great love for me. Because of that love, I don't have to judge the second half of my life by what has happened in the first half. Things are subject to change if you just lean on Jesus. When your human strength ends, God's super natural strength excels. It says in Philippians 3:13-15, "Brethren, I do not count myself to have apprehended; but one thing I do, forgetting those things which are behind and reaching forward to those things which are ahead, I press toward the goal for the prize of the upward call of God in Christ Jesus." It's hard to move forward when you keep the past in the present. Paul's Past was full with actions for which he was ashamed. Can you imagine what a loss it would have been to the body of Christ if Paul stayed stuck in his past offenses and not moved on to what God had for him? Don't get hung up with your hang ups. That was then and this is now! Let past hurts go. Whether you have suffered physical or emotional abuse, you must confront it then let it go! If you don't the pain lies dormant until triggered by something unexpected and the results are not pretty. That's why you may find yourself striking out at someone and later wondering where that came from. I took so much garbage into my present marriage; my husband should have walked away. But instead he loved me through my pain. It is important to marry someone that is a Believer. He prayed for me when I didn't have the strength to pray for myself. And most importantly he reminded me of the Blood of Jesus.

You need to understand the power of the Blood of Jesus that covers you. Your past is under the Blood. You don't have to keep bringing it up, or allowing anyone else to dredge it up. It has been dealt with by the Blood. We have overcome by the blood of the Lamb, Jesus Christ, and the word of our testimony. Through the blood of Jesus, and our witness of it, we overcome and have power to give our life fully for the One who gave His life for us. We apply the blood by the word of our testimony. According to Isaiah 53:5, "But He was wounded for our transgressions, He was bruised for our iniquities: The chastisement for our peace was upon him, and by His stripes we are healed."

You can apply the blood of Jesus to your body to receive your healing. You can apply the blood of Jesus to your mind, to receive a sound mind. You can apply the blood of Jesus to anyone and anything that you have authority over or influence upon. It is your right as God's child. Also in obedience to God's Holy Spirit you should apply the blood of Jesus to anything or anyone that He tells you to. It is your duty as a royal priest of the most High God. 1st Peter 2:9 says, "But you are a chosen generation, a royal priesthood, a holy nation, His own special people, that you may proclaim the praises of Him who called you out of darkness into His marvelous light." Why would God allow Jesus to suffer and die and then not give us what He suffered and died for? Because I have received Jesus as my Lord and Savior, I am no longer a slave to Satan. Jesus has set me free! You too are free, if you have accepted Jesus. We need to receive what Jesus has already paid for. It is ours! You have been forgiven; it is time to forgive others and most importantly to forgive yourself.

Finally, don't base your life on all the negative information fed to you from past relationships or parents, peers and even some preachers. I know the effect of that, having spent a large portion of my life trying to get other people's approval. You can get so wrapped up in trying to be what others expect you to be that you lose yourself. I have been there. I know what it feels like to be put down, to feel like you are nobody, to feel unwanted and all alone and all you have is you. So you try to fit in to a plan that was never designed for you in the first place, but I also know what it feels like to have peace, that peace which surpasses all understanding. I know what it feels like to have joy unspeakable and full of glory. I know what it feels like to have a Father who loves me. To be able to look myself in the mirror and say God loves me, God loves me! He looked beyond all my faults and saw my need, and He loves me!

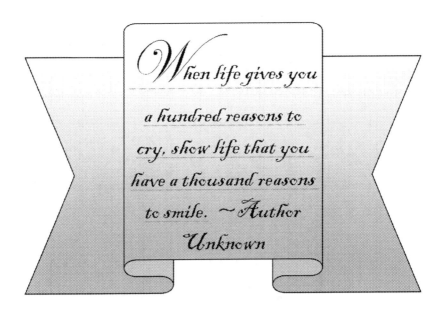

When life gives you a hundred reasons to cry, show life that you have a thousand reasons to smile. ~Author Unknown

CHAPTER EIGHT

Quitting Is Not an Option

Chapter Eight

Quitting Is Not an Option

Isaiah 61: 1-4: "The Spirit of the LORD God is upon me, Because the LORD has anointed me to preach good tidings to the poor; Has sent me to heal the brokenhearted, to proclaim liberty to the captives, and the opening of the prison to those who are bound; To proclaim the acceptable year of the LORD, and the day of vengeance of our God; To comfort all who mourn, To console those who mourn in Zion, To give them beauty for ashes, The oil of joy for mourning, The garment of praise for the spirit of heaviness; That they may be called trees of righteousness, The planting of the LORD, that He may be glorified. And they shall rebuild the old, They shall raise up the former desolations, and they shall repair the ruined cities, The desolations of many generations."

You can feel so lost when you have heard the Word of God and His promises and feel as though you don't have what you need for those promises to be released in you. What do you do when it seems like you have waited and waited and nothing happens? What do you do when you see people around you moving forward and you seem to be at a standstill? What do you do when you get past one thing and before you can take a deep breath here comes something else to taunt you?

Divorced and trying to hold things down as a single Mom can be trying. I have always wanted my daughters to know there was always something better over the horizon. I wanted them to never stop dreaming and no matter what else was going on we had each other. I would ask them, "how much do I love you?" and they would reply, "bigger than the whole wide world," and we would hug. They are my greatest accomplishment. How blessed I am to have their love. We have gone through many tough times together. I remember our car being repossessed and my job was about 6 miles from our home. I was working then as an assistant manager of a convenience store. My hours were three in the afternoon, until eleven at night. I would walk to work and after closing walk home at night praying all the way home. I did this for nearly three months until God opened another door for me. I thank God for the Angels watching over me, because I had no business on that dark road that time of the night alone. However, it was while working in that store I met someone who helped me get my next car and job.

You need to know that even when things seem bad, they can still work out for your good. Rest assured if God promised He will deliver. You just have to hold on to the Word until it becomes alive inside you. Don't quit! Quitting is not an option. God has orchestrated the events of your life for good.

Even when people have counted you out and thought you would never be back, out of the ashes of adversity comes resilience, commitment, strategy and tenacity. My father in the ministry use to tell us we had to have bull dog tenacity. You have to get hold to the Word for your situation and refuse to let it go!

You need to know that God does change lives. When God told Paul in 2 Cor. 12:9, "My grace is sufficient for you." He was saying that my Power is not intimidated by your circumstances. He has power to transcend your human limitations. Paul was able to do what he did because of the grace of God on his life. When I stopped trying to walk in my own head knowledge and trying to reason why things were the way they were, I was able to get in position so God's grace could transform me. I could prepare for the awesome future He has for me and stop living in the past. You too can have the future that God has designed for you. Don't allow the enemy to get you off course. There are many of you who should be lenders have been reduced to perpetual borrowers; those destined to be leaders have been sidelined to just followers; many who are suppose to enjoy their marriages have been plagued with frequent divorce and remarriage, or because you don't feel worthy jump from one bed to another; and the list goes on. Why? Because you settled! You saw yourself in the eyes of your past instead of in the eyes of our God. But it is not too late. I am a living witness that it is not too late.

I encourage you to find that for which God has called you to and pursue it. If you don't, you may find yourself living out someone else's dream and never living yours. 2 Peter 1:10 says, "Therefore, brethren, be even more diligent to make your call and election sure, for if you do these things you will never stumble." You can not fail doing what God has called you to do. There is no failure in God. His plans are already blessed. When God speaks a thing, it is what He says it is. That's why you should find what the word says about your situation and stand on it. Never let go of the promises of God. In spite of what you see, keep the word in your heart and meditate on it and keep feeding your faith. We have to be consistent with the word not on and off.

God is waiting for us to take hold of His promises by faith and begin living the life He has designed just for us. It is hard to believe while you are going through difficulties that the things you go through help develop you for your purpose. Your test gives you a testimony. There are some things you may go through, that no one else can go through with you. Sometimes you don't need to be around anyone's influence but the Holy Spirits'. Stop feeling like you need everyone's approval of you. The only approval that you need is God's. Everything I need to accomplish what God has called me to do is already in me. Everything you need is already in you. Don't spend years like I did comparing to other people. Don't allow your past to distort who you really are. Nobody can beat you at being you. You are alright just the way God designed you. You are perfect for your purpose and destiny. There is a creative Word waiting to give birth to something great on the inside of you!

When everything seems to be against you,
remember that the airplane takes off against the
wind, not with it. – Henry Ford

CHAPTER NINE

Break the Secrecy

Chapter Nine

Break the Secrecy

When you have been abused, it is easier to keep it inside and not talk about it. You do not have to feel ashamed. It was not your fault. If you are presenting being abused tell someone! You also have the authority to give that demonic spirit of abuse a restraining order. It is trespassing on God's property. God does not abuse His children and neither does he want them abused. There are parts of my childhood I can't remember. I believe it is my minds self defense mechanism. There is a release when you finally talk to someone. You could not as a child process how to deal with feelings of hopelessness or anger but as an adult you have to fight and defend the child within you.

Once you are free, break the silence! Expose Satan, he can only work in the dark. He is powerless when confronted with the light. He will tell you to keep it covered up so people won't judge you. Or he asks you the question; what will those close to you think if they knew? What about your reputation? Suppose no one believes you? Whether you are the abused or the abuser, you need to uncover it so healing can take place.

Transparency is not easy. It is not easy, especially if you are in a "religious church" to relax in the freedom you have after repentance. God forgives us but sometimes "religion" wants to keep you in bondage. Ever been to a Church and listened to the Minister tell you how saved he was? You get the impression he has never done anything wrong since he was converted at the age of nine. You ask yourself how can he relate to me as messed up as I am? So what happens? You cover your scars so no one can see from hence you have come. You hear the whispers as they talk about someone else in the church realizing that if they only knew that could be you.

I recall being asked to speak at a church when I was real young in the ministry. It was a huge church with a large congregation. It was the church of one of my former professors. Their church was quiet and conservative. I felt honored speaking to this group of whom I knew were mostly well established professionals in the community. I had written a nice "speech" that I felt suited this well dressed audience.

After being introduced, I stood at the podium and carefully placed my notes. Immediately, I heard the Holy Spirit say, "put those notes away. I want you to give them your testimony." No, I thought. There is no way I am going to do that. Not with this audience especially. I was having an internal battle and in no uncertain term was I doing that. Now that I had settled that, I took a deep breath and prepared to speak. I opened my mouth nothing came out! I tried once again to speak and nothing would come out. The audience was staring at me and I was feeling more and more embarrassed by the minute. Finally in desperation I screamed out, "Ok. Lord you win!" I could speak again! I looked at all the people in front of me and with tears in my eyes asked for their forgiveness. I explained that I had come to give me what I had planned for them but God had another plan. He wanted me to share with them my testimony. As I begin to share I felt a release in my spirit that was long over due.

When the service was over a young woman walked up to me and hugged me crying. "Thank you, I had told the Lord that I was tired but I was going to give him one more chance to speak to me. I came to this service as a last hope, because my plan was to leave here and to go home and kill myself." I could feel a lump in my stomach as she told me her story. Lord, forgive me, I thought. My disobedience could have cost someone their life! That taught me a lesson I will never forget. My secrecy was not worth a life. The test we go through should serve as a testimony so others can also be free. I found out that night there was several people who had secrets that haunted them. You can not look at a person and tell who they really are. Behind the mask you may find anything.

The little girl on the inside of me had been crying out and I had kept her silent. After all she must have been a bad girl, why else had she been punished? It is hard to be the person you have been designed to be when the child on the inside has never been given an opportunity to deal with the pain of growing up. Not dealing with it will lead to unstable relationships. Find someone you can trust and talk about what you are feeling. When the devil is exposed he will flee.

When we don't expose it you are left to deal with the devil's lies which tell you that no matter what relationship you are in you will be treated badly. So instead of enjoying the relationship you are waiting for the other shoe to fall. Your partner will not have a chance when you are already expecting him or her to be just like all the rest. You will never have peace, joy or happiness in life until you deal with the little child crying out inside of you. Set that child free and love yourself so you can be free to love and be loved. However, it is so much easier to say than to do. Letting go can be hard, especially when you have held on so long to your past hurts. We had heard preachers say to name it and claim it and want to believe it's just that simple. However, something triggers a past memory and you find yourself slipping back into that dark place full of pain and disappointment. You can only be a prisoner to what you won't confront. That's why it is so important to expose the secrecy.

It is time to allow your inner child to come out of the dark shadows of fear and pain. Never again allow that child to be dismissed and made to feel insufficient. What the inner child has to say is important. It took me years to give my inner child a voice. With God's love as our foundation, we can now hold hands and walk into our future together.

Put yourself in a state of mind where you say to yourself, "Here is an opportunity for me to celebrate like never before, my own power, my own ability to get myself to do whatever is necessary. – Martin Luther King

CHAPTER TEN

Will I Ever Be Free

Chapter Ten

Will I Ever Be Free

**"Therefore if the Son makes you free you shall be free
indeed."
John 8:36**

God does not want us in bondage to anything. He wants us free. The devil would like nothing better than to keep you in bondage. The Word of God tells us Satan is a thief, murderer, and destroyer, all rolled up in one. Let's make sure we understand this: God is not in the oppression business, He is in the "freedom" business. You have a choice now, to either stay in unforgiveness and pain over the past or receive the Freedom that awaits you by turning it all over to Jesus. There is liberty in turning your cares over to the Lord.

I encourage you; don't give anyone that much power over your life by holding on to unforgiveness. If you give them that power, you'll end up miserable and that person will be moving on with their life like you never existed. Say a prayer for the person and ask God to release all the hate in your heart so that you can move on. If you don't, you'll never be able to trust another relationship or open your heart to one. You're allowing someone to steal your happiness and they don't deserve that type of victory over you.

There is little that affects our relationships so profoundly and adversely as an unforgiving spirit. Holding something against someone has a tendency to dominate our lives. We may not even realize it. We think we have it resolved in our minds. But all the time it is eating away at us, affecting our disposition, our physical health, and unquestionably affecting the way we treat the people who reach out to us.

Every time you remember how you've been hurt, release it. You must decide to let go. When Jesus was asked how often we should forgive someone who sins against us, he said 70 times seven. Or in other words, we just keep forgiving.

The truth is, if you don't release the person who has hurt you, then you will resemble him. Whatever you focus on, you'll become like. If you focus on pain, that's what you move toward. If you focus on the life God has prepared for you, your life will move in that direction.

Have faith that a better future has already been prepared for you. Faith does not give your flesh or your natural circumstances a vote. Your mind set has to be fixed not on your faith, but on the God of your faith. We have to silence every voice in our mind except that of the Lord. It is no disgrace to need help. Pray for someone who can be a support for you. Let the Holy Spirit help you. Allow the Holy Spirit to restore you. Nothing has a greater authority than the Word that God has already decreed.

I had to come to the reality that the past can't change. The important thing is I am a survivor. If you have gone through any type of abuse and are still here to tell it Glory to God! You have strength you don't even realize on the inside of you. Take charge of those feelings that make you feel like a victim and speak to them in the Name of Jesus and tell they have no place in your future. You may have no control over what happened then, but you do have control of how you will walk out your future.

Fight to hold on to the freedom we have in Jesus Christ. It is a fight that you can win because over two thousand years ago He took your weakness and gave you His strength. He took your sin and gave you His righteousness. He had already won the battle for you and taken every defeat and made you a victor instead of a victim.

There were points in my life where I thought I was free and had moved on until something happened or was said that just seemed to trigger those past and hurtful emotions. One of the cruelest things is to have someone whom you confided in to say to you "just get over it." Do you think that if it was that easy, the person would have already moved pass it? How many people do you know that would like to relive abuse of any kind over and over again? Yet, many people do. You lose the ability to really trust people. You wonder what their motive is, even if they do something thoughtful. The reality of it is nothing can bring us back into wholeness but the Blood of Jesus.

It was during one of these times I cried out to the Lord and I could hear Him say to me, "Broken Vessels can be mended." It was there in my quiet time that the Father spoke to me about ministering to broken vessels. "Lord I'm broken," I said. And He told me, "as you minister to others I will minister to you. As you meet the needs of others, I will meet your needs. As you cry before me for others, I will anoint your tears, for their deliverance." That birthed in my heart the "Broken Vessels Can Be Mended" conferences.

In Conclusion

In conclusion of writing this book, I want to say that, what you can walk away from, you have mastered. What you cannot walk away from, has mastered you. God has a glorious future for you, but you can't go into it holding on to the past.

Philippians 3:13-14, "Brethren, I do not count myself to have apprehended; but one thing I do, forgetting those things which are behind and reaching forward to those things which are ahead, I press toward the goal for the prize of the upward call of God in Christ Jesus."

Find that thing for which God has called you to and walk in it. Begin to dream again and don't let past decisions or hurts stop you from pressing forward. If fact, be an instrument God can use to help someone else. Walk out your deliverance by helping someone else walk out theirs. Don't be weighed down with what you cannot change. Hebrew 12: 1-2, "Therefore we also, since we are surrounded by so great a cloud of witnesses, let us lay aside every weight, and the sin which so easily ensnares us, and let us run with endurance the race that is set before us, Looking unto Jesus the author and finisher of our faith, who for the joy that was set before him endured the cross, despising the shame, and has sat down at the right hand of the throne of God." You can make it. I'm living proof!

If you have not entered into a committed relationship with Christ, I invite you to do so right now. You don't have to wait until you get to church. Where you are right now you can make Jesus the Lord of your life. Salvation can be yours right now. Let's pray:

> Father God, I am a sinner. I believe that Jesus is
> the Son of God.
> I believe that he died for my sins and that he rose
> again from the dead.
> I invite Jesus to come into my life. I receive the
> price he paid for my sin
> and accept him as my Savior and Lord
> Amen

Welcome to the family of God! I encourage you to find a Christ centered Church, who considers the Bible the final authority. We will be happy to help you find a Church in your area. It is your season to experience God's best!

Resources

Unless otherwise indicated all scriptures are from the King James Version of the Bible.

If you would like to support this ministry, receive our ministry tapes, get the locations of speaking engagements, or would like us to come to minister, please write to:

Evangelist Kayla Johnson

Free & Restored Evangelistic Ministries

P.O. Box 580890
Kissimmee, Florida 34758

Email us: kaylak208@aol.com
www.freeandrestored.com

Please send us your prayer request.
We want to come into agreement with your needs
as we stand together on the Word of God.

Appendix I

What Is Domestic Violence?

According to the National Abuse Hotline

Domestic violence can be defined as a pattern of behavior in any relationship that is used to gain or maintain power and control over an intimate partner.

Abuse is physical, sexual, emotional, economic, or psychological actions or threats of actions that influence another person. This includes any behaviors that frighten, intimidate, terrorize, manipulate, hurt, humiliate, blame, injure or wound someone.

Domestic violence can happen to anyone of any age, race, sexual orientation, religion or gender. It can happen to couples who are married, living together or who are dating. Domestic violence affects people of all socioeconomic backgrounds and education levels.

You may be in an emotionally abusive relationship if your partner:

- Calls you names, insults you or continually criticizes you
- Does not trust you and acts jealous or possessive
- Tries to isolate you from family or friends
- Monitors where you go, who you call and who you spend time with
- Does not want you to work
- Controls finances or refuses to share money
- Punishes you by withholding affection
- Expects you to ask permission
- Threatens to hurt you, the children, your family or your pets
- Humiliates you in any way

You may be in a physically abusive relationship if your partner has ever:

- Damaged property when angry (thrown objects, punched walls, kicked doors, etc.)
- Pushed, slapped, bitten, kicked or choked you
- Abandoned you in a dangerous or unfamiliar place
- Scared you by driving recklessly
- Used a weapon to threaten or hurt you
- Forced you to leave your home
- Trapped you in your home or kept you from leaving
- Prevented you from calling police or seeking medical attention
- Hurt your children
- Used physical force in sexual situations

You may be in a sexually abusive relationship if your partner:

- Views women as objects and believes in rigid gender roles
- Accuses you of cheating or is often jealous of your outside relationships
- Wants you to dress in a sexual way
- Insults you in a sexual way or calls you sexual names
- Has ever forced or manipulated you into having sex or performing sexual acts
- Held you down during sex
- Demanded sex when you were sick, tired or after beating you
- Hurt you with weapons or objects during sex
- Involved other people in sexual activities with you
- Ignored your feelings regarding sex

If you answered "yes" to these questions you may be in an abusive relationship; please call the National Domestic Violence Hotline at 1-800-799-SAFE (7233), 1-800-787-3224 (TTY) or your local domestic violence center to talk with someone about it.

Appendix II

Scriptures for Forgiveness

When we burden ourselves with anger, hate, and vengeance, we forfeit the blessings of having the guidance of the Holy Spirit.

Matthew 5:44-47 KJV: "But I say to you, love your enemies, bless those who curse you, do good to those who hate you, and pray for those who spitefully use you and persecute you,[a] 45 that you may be sons of your Father in heaven; for He makes His sun rise on the evil and on the good, and sends rain on the just and on the unjust. 46 For if you love those who love you, what reward have you? Do not even the tax collectors do the same? 47 And if you greet your brethren[b] only, what do you do more *than others?* Do not even the tax collectors do so?"

Leviticus 19:18 KJV: "You shall not take vengeance, nor bear any grudge against the children of your people, but you shall love your neighbor as yourself: I *am* the LORD."

Luke 6:37-38 KJV: "Judge not, and you shall not be judged. Condemn not, and you shall not be condemned. Forgive, and you will be forgiven. 38 Give, and it will be given to you: good measure, pressed down, shaken together, and running over will be put into your bosom. For with the same measure that you use, it will be measured back to you."

There are really two parts to forgiveness: first, our relationship to God; and second, our relationship to the other person.

Colossians 3:13 KJV: "Bearing with one another, and forgiving one another, if anyone has a complaint against another; even as Christ forgave you, so you also *must do.*

Endnotes

Preface
    1. Proverbs 4:20-22
    2. Romans 8:1-3

Chapter One
    1. 1 Samuel 12:24
    2. Psalms 30:5b
    3. Romans 8:31
    4. Jeremiah 1:5-8
    5. Source: Attitude is Everything, by Francie Baltazar-
        Schwartz http://www.bluinc.com/free/bullet.htm (1998)

Chapter Two
    Luke 22:31-32
    Luke 10:19
    Luke 22: 1-6

Chapter Three
    Mark 11:25-26
    2 Cor, 10:5
    Mat. 16:22
    John 10:4-5
    Psalms 84:11
    Ephesians 3: 20

Chapter Four
    1 Cor. 10:13
    Gen. 4:8
    Gen. 9:21
    Gen. 19:30-38
    Gen. 30:14-16

Gen. 37:3-28

2 Sam. 12:9-12
Mark3:21
Romans 5: 6-8
Jeremiah 29:11
I Corinthians 2:9
Chapter Five
Romans 8:18
Jeremiah 29:13
John 4:6-18
1 Corinthians 15:3
Psalms 42:1,2
Matthew 11:28
Deut 30:19

Chapter Six
John 5: 5-9
3 John 2
Jeremiah 17:14
Psalm 34:19
1 John 4:17
1 Corinthians 6:15-17
Romans 3:4
Hosea 4:6

Chapter Seven
Philippians 4:13
Philip. 3:13-15
Isaiah 53:5
Peter 2:9

Chapter Eight
Isaiah 61: 1-4
2 Cor. 12:9
2 Peter 1:10

"*Forgiveness* . . . allows the love of God to purge your heart and mind of the poison of hate. It cleanses your consciousness of the desire for revenge. It makes place for the purifying, healing, restoring love of the Lord" (in Conference Report, Apr. 1992, 45; or *Ensign*, May 1992, 33)

Personal Journal

I became ill, holding so much inside. I don't want that for you. Here is your opportunity not to go through what I went through. Use the following pages to express the things you have wanted to say and felt you didn't know how. There is no one on these pages to judge you and no one to hear the secrets you have held onto so long. So now it's time to let it all go!

Afterwards, take a deep breath. Now tear these pages out and then destroy them symbolic of a new beginning. I wish you the best and I pray that today will be the first day of the rest of the life God intended for you.

Journal

The secret I have held onto for so long is _____

_____

_____

_____

_____

_____

_____

_____

I felt I could not tell it because _____

_____

_____

_____

_____

_____

_____

I will no longer allow it to hold me a prisoner. I now release those who have hurt or disappointed me by faith in the Name of Jesus. These are the names of those I now release and what it is I release them from

_____

_____

_____

_____

_____

_____

_____

_____

_____

_____

I now pray for the following people living or dead and forgive them and ask that you forgive them also.

_____

_____

_____

_____

_____

_____

_____

_____

_____

I am now free to live my life. This is what I want the rest of my life to look like

_____

_____

_____

_____

_____

_____

_____

_____

_____

_____

_____

_____

_____

_____

_____

_____

_____

_____

_____

_____

_____

_____

Personal Diary

Kayla D. Johnson

_____
_____
_____
_____
_____
_____
_____
_____
_____
_____
_____
_____
_____
_____
_____
_____
_____
_____
_____
_____
_____
_____
_____
_____
_____
_____
_____
_____
_____
_____
_____
_____
_____
_____
_____

Kayla D. Johnson

Kayla D. Johnson